Bible stories & prayers for pregnancy and early motherhood.

You're Not Alone

Candice Jenee'

YOU'RE NOT ALONE:

Bible Stories & Prayers for pregnancy and early motherhood.

Candice Jenee'
Tiny Nephesh Ministry

YOU'RE NOT ALONE: BIBLE STORIES & PRAYERS
FOR PREGNANCY AND EARLY MOTHERHOOD

Published by: Candice Jeneé @ Tiny Nephesh Ministry
Tulsa, Oklahoma
http://tinynephesh.com

ISBN 13: 978-0-9848555-7-5 (Paperback)

CONTENTS

GET 3 MORE STORIES AND PRAYERS FOR FREE!

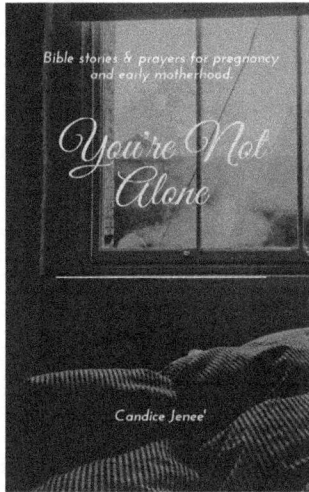

go to https://tinynephesh.com/free-updates-2/yourenotalone
to get access to 3 more stories for free today!

NOTES OF THANKS:

To my momma, thank you for praying for me by name before I was ever known. Thank you for all of your support these past 30+ years. I would not be the woman or mother I am today without your faithfulness, your love, and your prayer. Remember: I'll love you forever.

To my cousin Melinda, thank you for being the first to invest in this project. And, for believing in me no matter what I take on. I have enjoyed learning from you and growing to become friends. We may be miles apart now, but I'm glad God blessed me with a cousin and friend as great as you.

To my best friend Jamie, I'm so glad we got to go through this pregnancy time together. What a blessing. Thank you for the talks and wisdom. Your kiddos are blessed with an amazing momma.

And, finally, to my Baby Girl, thanks for making me a momma. What a wild ride it has been. I thank God for you every day.

YOU'RE NOT ALONE
- DAY 1

Introduction

If this book has found its way to you, I'd guess you are pregnant or recently became a momma - whether for the first time or the 20th time.

Often times, pregnancy and early motherhood can feel isolating and lonely. At least, it had been for me and several of my friends. And, while I do feel blessed to have other pregnant and new mommas around me, so many days and nights it can get extremely, desperately lonely.

As I looked for books or devotionals for this time, what I found just wasn't what I was hoping for or wanting. Whether stating I shouldn't be sick and uncomfortable during pregnancy because I'm redeemed (which isn't a Biblical picture of redemption, by the way), or just brushing the surface of everything, or simply having too much overwhelming information and commitment - it just wasn't what I needed.

I felt like there was something deeper - something more to learn and connect to Biblically. To connect with from women in the Bible. More to pray. More to build community around. So, God placed it on my heart to write it, because He impressed upon me that I wasn't the only one.

Along the way, I have been studying different women of the Bible. God has been showing me that not only am I not alone now, but historically - from Eve to Mary and beyond – I'm not alone.

And, neither are you. Not in the loneliness. Not in the infertility. Not in the single motherhood. Not in the discomfort. Not in the questions. Not in the excitement. Not in the joy. Not in the prayers. Not in the pain. Not in the loss.

We are not alone. Even in the lowest, loneliest time.

This book is for you and it was born out of this realization:

WE are not alone.

You're Not Alone

Here on day 1, I'd like to invite you to sit in the fact that you are not alone - even though you might feel it. Spend a few minutes letting that sink into your spirit. I have days I still don't feel it. Days I still feel completely and utterly alone. But, I know it to be true *that I am not alone.* Allow this to become truth for you:

You are not alone.

Over the next 16 days, I'll introduce you to the Biblical women who went before; and I'll give you prayers and verses for this precious time.

At the end, you'll find a quick reference guide of verses to just come back to when needed throughout this beautiful, blessed and breathtaking journey.

One last thought I'd like you to allow to sink in during this time is that Psalm 139 isn't just about David. And, it isn't just about you.

Right now, if you are pregnant, God is weaving your baby together in your womb. If you just had a baby, God knew that baby before they were born. God knows the number of hairs that already exist. He knows the number of new hairs you got in pregnancy and the number of hairs you'll lose postpartum (and trust me, it will be a lot). The God of miracles, second chances, and no mistakes, is the God who is creating life in you now, and who has chosen you to carry the blessing of motherhood.

Day 1 - Prayer

Abba:

Thank you for this blessing. Thank you for allowing me to be a part of the miracle of creation.

You see my heart. You know all of the range of feelings - both physical and emotional - that I have. During the sad, lonely, and broken times, please give me peace and grace. On the days of excitement and joy, help me keep that going.

As I go forward in the next 16 days, may I really learn that I am not alone. Send a mom community I can connect with. Connect me with what Your word says about womanhood, pregnancy, and motherhood, as well as the women who came before.

Thank you again for this blessing. I am so excited to be a part of this creation miracle. I am so blessed and honored to be so.

Amen.

EVE - THE FIRST MOMMA

From Scripture

"To the woman he said, "I will make your pain in childbearing very severe; with pain you will give birth to children. Your desire will be for your husband and he will rule over you."" - Genesis 3:16

Learning from Eve

Ah, the garden. Where it all began. The whole world. And, the source of our pain in childbirth. Now, some women LOVE being pregnant, every minute of it. Some women, like me, only get to enjoy it for a few brief minutes due to being sick for 9 months, and everything in between. Either way, we all seem to have that one thing we focus on. For me, it was baby kicks. Honestly, I miss those some days.

But, back to our friend Eve.

Eve was the first momma. Though before this moment, we don't know what childbearing was supposed to be like, but we were still created to bring forth life. It is our beautiful role in creation (one of many we bear). What we do know about life before that fateful fall is that Eve was created for Adam, and that God had already designed a plan for human multiplication. He even gave them a command to multiply.

If I'm being honest, when I think about Eve, I often focus on that stupid fruit. I used to hold Eve in contempt because my "pain in childbearing" began with puberty. As a PMDD sufferer, my symp-

5

toms are physical & emotional. I also have some other lingering issues I'm reminded of month after month, and at one time, I blamed Eve. After revisiting her story, I see she has already borne the consequences of her own actions greatly.

You see, as the first momma, Eve experienced every facet of the childbearing and raising process:

- Pregnancy and childbirth
- Raising children
- Losing a child to death
- Losing a child to poor actions
- Losing her home
- A child born after loss

Eve had to walk through each of these situations. Something other mommas in this book experience, but she lived through them all. Imagine burying Abel, or watching Cain have to leave the garden. Imagine looking into Seth's eyes after saying goodbye to two others. Imagine the heartbreak she already carried as a result of her choice.

No, Eve doesn't need me to crucify her with the burden I now bear. She bore it all on her own.

From today's verse, though, we learn that this side of heaven, childbearing won't be easy. For some, it is. Honestly, though pregnancy and postpartum have rocked my world, labor and delivery were extremely smooth. It's different for everyone. But, we have the promise that it won't, generally, come easily. It is an often uncomfortable and painful process. I can only imagine it would have been for Eve, the first momma. And, how much scarier, having no one who had gone before her?

Lucky for us, the difficulty and pain does not erase the joy that comes with being an active part in God's creation. God has given us the beautiful burden of partnering with Him in the creation process.

Revisiting Eve's story has given me a compassion for her, and for

Candice Jeneé

other mommas.

And she is my greatest proof that I am not alone in this childbearing and rearing journey, no matter the outcome.

Eve's prayer

Abba:

Thank you for choosing me to be the mother of my baby. Thank you for the burden of partnering with you in creation. No matter what the journey looks like, whether all roses or a bed of thorns, may I never forget the joy that is being a mother. Lord, I don't know what life You have ahead for my child, but I pray that I would be an excellent example and source of love for all of my children. May the grace You have shown me flow through me to them, even in my most sleep-deprived or uncomfortable stage.

God, thank you that even in the midst of the "fallen", I still get a glimpse of redemption by holding a baby who had just been close to Your heart, then sat under my heart, and then in my arms.

Please, send me other mommas to experience this journey with. May we support each other in ways Eve was never blessed to have. Thank you for all the mommas who went before me.

Lord, my baby and my motherhood journey are Yours.

Amen.

Further Reading

Genesis 2-4

SARAH - AGE IS JUST A NUMBER

From Scripture

"Sarah said, "God has brought me laughter, and everyone who hears about this will laugh with me." And she added, "Who would have said to Abraham that Sarah would nurse children? Yet I have borne him a son in his old age."" - Genesis 21:6-7

Learning from Sarah

There is so much about Sarah and pregnancy/motherhood we could learn *not* to do: losing faith in God's word, being manipulative and abusive to others, lying, becoming bitter, trading God's plans for ours, etc.

However, we're going to focus on her age and life stage. Sarah was "advanced in age". This is the main reason she laughed at God. By "advanced in years", scripture means she was late in life, likely 90s! Sarah and Abraham had no kids, but God made them a promise to make their descendants like the grains of sand on the beach. Sarah actually laughed at the notion. In her age, it's no wonder she was skeptical. In today's world, our pregnancies get classified as "geriatric" if they happen at 35 years or later.

However, also in today's world, we are able to sustain pregnancy at older ages, even well into our 40s. If you find yourself an older momma, you are definitely not alone. The crowd of over 30 women having babies grows every year. These women have lived lives before having babies. They have already lived 10+ years of adulthood, and may have prayed and prayed for their babies. Or, maybe they thought they were done with babies and God surprised them. Maybe, they got custody of grand kids and are starting all over Whatever way it happens, age does not preclude us from being able to carry and/or raise our children.

Honestly, getting married in my late 20s, I was worried about not having kids until my 30s. Part of me was worried: *could I keep up with babies? What would happen as they got older?* I do have a great example of being able to keep up in later motherhood, as my mom was in her 30s with both of my little sisters, but still. These thoughts plagued me.

If you have concerns about this, you are most certainly not alone. I read the blogs, the forums, the Facebook pages. Women were wondering if they'd be able to get pregnant, if their pregnancies would be viable, if their babies would be ok, if they would be able to keep up. Rejoicing over the expected blessing and worrying about the life change ahead. I have sat with clients when I was doing therapy who got custody of grandkids and found themselves starting over, wondering if they could make it work in a new system.

God knows us, He knew the age we'd be when we became mothers (for the first or fifteenth time...). He entrusted us with these babies, planned them just for us. He sent them in His perfect timing, just like He did for Sarah. God's promise is always sure and true. His blessings come even though we don't deserve them, but He knows the right time for them in our lives.

Sarah ended up naming her Son after her laughter. And, aside from being abusive toward Hagar, we seem to see Sarah as an honorable, faithful wife and mother in the rest of her story. She is Abraham's partner, and raises a son who honors God.

Just as we should be with our blessings. Accepting of God's timing, and raising them in Him. No matter what age we are when the blessing comes.

Sarah's Prayer

Abba:

Thank you for my precious gift. Mid-life seems so late to have a baby, but Your timing is perfect. I know that you have called me to be a momma to this baby. I pray for a smooth pregnancy and delivery, and that I would have supernatural energy to be the momma You've called me to be.

I know age is just a number in so many ways. I also know that if you call me to this at this stage, You will see me through it for as many years as they are with me. You are the equipper and sustainer.

Thank you for a support system as I figure out how to raise a baby at this stage of life.

Amen.

Further Reading

Genesis 16-18; Genesis 21

HAGAR - SINGLE MOMMA

From Scripture

"The angel of the Lord also said to her: "You are now pregnant and you will give birth to a son. You shall name him Ishmael, for the lord has heard of your misery."" - Genesis 16:11

Learning from Hagar

This book includes a select few pregnancy and motherhood topics that I haven't experienced first-hand - but I felt moved they need to be included because we are each coming to motherhood from different places. This is one of those chapters, because, while I have a wonderful husband along side of me in this journey, not everyone does.

Hagar was not only a single momma, but she wasn't single by choice, nor did she have her baby by choice. And, she definitely had a lot of momma drama going on.

Her employer basically forced her to marry her husband out of a lack of trust in God. The union produced a child, and also produced an abusive and insecure boss. Hagar feared for her life and ran. She took her son into the desert. An angel sent her back, encouraging her that God was with her.

When her boss finally did have a baby, Hagar was forced away, to finish raising her child on her own. She was so desperate in one moment, she left her preteen son in a spot in the desert, and went quite a ways away from him to weep. *Why?* Because she had no food and water for him, and *she couldn't bear to watch him die.*

Guys, I can't even imagine the heartache this momma felt not being able to provide for her child. Desperate women do desperate things - single mommas trying to care for their kiddos are no different.

If you are doing this alone, I'm so sorry. This task is a big, life-consuming job, and if no one has told you lately, you're a rock star. You are the light in that baby's life.

The unfortunate thing is any of us could find ourselves there at a moment's notice for whatever reason. A while ago, my husband was in a car accident that totaled our car. Lucky for us, he only experienced major bruising - but boy was I terrified after that. It was a reminder that in an instant, I could have to take on this task alone.

Yet, there are many mommas out there already doing this task alone. They are working two jobs, they are trying to find child-care, they are making sure homework is done or food is on the table. They are trying to co-parent, or explain why their kiddos never see daddy (for whatever reason). If they are where they are due to life's cruelty, they may also be crying quiet tears to themselves when they miss their partner while trying to comfort a crying child.

But, single mommas are really some of the strongest people on the planet. I've only had to go three to four days at a time by myself, and it gave me the greatest respect for women who walk this path alone. But, remember, you aren't alone. Hagar was there, too. She knows the baby momma drama, the sharing a paternal figure, the "ugly stepmother", the being cut off with no support.

Yet, in the desert, God heard her. And, He blessed her. Today, God hears you, and He blesses you.

Hagar's Prayer

Abba:

Even though I seem to be doing this alone, I am not alone. You are with me always. You have never left my side, just like you didn't leave Hagar.

When I feel like I simply can't go on, when I have to take desperate action to make sure my baby has food or clothes, when I miss my lost partner, I pray for peace. When I feel anger well up at being left or forgotten, I pray for forgiveness to flood my heart. I pray You would remind me that you haven't left me, wrap me in Your comforting love and grace. When I feel I have nothing left to give, may I wake up and press on one more day.

I know this baby you have given me is a blessing, no matter the circumstances. This child did not choose this timing and is not to blame. May their love and laughter keep me soft and tender.

Amen

Further Reading

Genesis 16-18; Genesis 21

REBEKAH - TWINS!

From Scripture

"So they called Rebekah and asked her, "Will you go with this man?" "I will go," she said." - Genesis 24:58

Learning from Rebekah

Rebekah amazes me with her willingness; her faithfulness to God's plan. Not only did it lead her away from her family into a strange land and into the arms of a man she'd never met, but it led to twins. Twins!

This is another area where I am not an expert. Not only do I not have a set of multiples, but I only have one baby right now. However, I didn't want to leave moms of multiples out of this book, because, you're represented too, and you are the real MVPs. Rebekah is right there with you (as Tamar will be). Birthing two babies, caring for two babies, dividing attention between two babies. All at once.

I don't know how y'all do it with two or three or more at a time. One has me on my toes always, and leaves me feeling the exhaustion.

That said, I do know the stress of divided attention. When our babies - no matter how many there are - are in our bellies, they have all of us for those 9 months. They have our attention, they are with us 24/7. Our bodies are at their beck and call at all times. Once we give birth, that's no longer true, no matter how many babies we have.

Candice Jeneé

I know what it's like to need a minute: to cook or clean or even go to the bathroom, and you can't be focused on that baby all the time. I can only imagine what it's like with more than one. You have to divide attention between those babies *and* any other tasks you may have.

Rebekah must have known how this felt. Two babies. Two mouths to feed. Two meals to make. Two babies to try to entertain and keep calm while she also had to, you know, cook or clean or go to the bathroom. I can imagine how easy it would be to get overwhelmed in that situation, and how on your game you'd have to be.

One thing I do love about Rebekah is her willingness. She is willing to leave everything when Abraham's servant tells her why he is in the land to begin with, that he is there to find a wife for Isaac. She is willing to marry a man she's never met. She is willing to fall in line into God's story. And, she is willing to bear & raise those twins.

Rebekah, unfortunately also picked a favorite, one she manipulated into getting the family blessing. So, that favorite became the blessed one, the one in whose line Christ was born. That favorite wrestled with God. But, he also went about a lot if it dishonestly at first. This was all before he was renamed, Israel. The one who God's chosen people would come from.

Like Rebekah, I'd also guess it's easy to pick a favorite. Though, I'd strongly encourage against this. I know it's only human nature to attach ourselves with those who are most like us. The same may be true for our children. And, we won't focus on it, but I wanted to bring the issue to attention for those of us who have or plan to have more than one child - however that might come about. Something to watch out for.

What I want to focus on is you, momma of multiples, momma of babies of different ages. Mommas willing to take on the task of mothering more than one baby, you are not alone. With Rebekah, you are in good company. She has walked the path of caring for more than one baby at a time, teaching two toddlers to walk, talk, and potty (though I'm sure the potty process looked so much different back then).

Those of you with your willing hearts to take on those sweet twins, triplets, or more, or those mommas whose babies are very close in age - I'm looking at you momma with 2 under 2 or 3 under 3 - that willing spirit is the same one Rebekah walked her life in. A willingness to fall in line with God's plan, which obviously includes you as the precious mothers to these precious babies. That's why He gave them to you.

You, tired momma with attention divided between home tasks, work, and multiple babies, you are not alone.

Rebekah's Prayer

Abba:

Thank you for my babies. All of them. Thank you for trusting me to take care of multiple precious kiddos. I may not have chosen myself for this task, but You have chosen me, so in You I know I am up to it.

God, give me energy and focus. Supernatural energy and focus that can only come from Your Spirit. It is so hard to make sure all of my attention and focus is in the right place when I have more than one baby to love on and pour into, but I also have a house to clean, food to prepare, and a husband who also rightly needs my attention and affection. I know my heart has enough room for all of it, but my body and mind are tired.

Lord, I am so in awe that You have chosen me for this task of motherhood. I am willing to take it on with honor.

Thank you.

Amen.

Candice Jeneé

Further Reading

Genesis 24-27

LEAH - FIERCE WOMANHOOD

From Scripture

"She conceived again, and when she gave birth to a son, she said, "This time I will praise the Lord." So she named him Judah..." - Genesis 29:35

Learning from Leah

For most of my life, I have related to Leah. From having two gorgeous younger sisters (seriously, they are knock-outs) to life events when I was younger that instilled I was possibly: unlovable, unwanted, an inconvenience (all lies, I know, but feelings I have felt before). I was in my late 20s before my husband came into my life and showed me that kind of love. A love Leah never got to experience. (Don't worry, my husband loves me & never went after my sisters. They have their own Godly men, and I couldn't be prouder. But, they are seriously gorgeous).

Leah was one who was overlooked, she was unwanted. She was, by cultural standards, unacceptable and seemingly unlovable. Her father had to trick Jacob into marrying her.

But, in her story, I see a fierceness I see in few others. How is that? Through her story we see her go from:

- Unwanted and unloved to
- Determined and
- Misused to

- Fighter to
- Hurt and
- Temporarily allowing bitterness in to
- Choosing to stand on her own in God.

She finally chooses in the face of all of her adversity to stand on her own in God. She chooses the love of God and the love of her children, even without the love of her husband.

Leah was extremely blessed. She was also extremely tenacious. And, it is through her line that Christ comes. It is her son that gets the blessing, her son that saves Joseph from death, her son who is listed in that line of Christ - the Lion of Judah.

When I worry that my view of myself, my feeling of inadequacy, unlovability, or inconvenience, threaten to beat me down, I remember Leah's fierceness. It is a fierceness I want to relate to.

Her ability to stand in God and raise her children is something I aspire to. I just hope to get there a little quicker than she did.

By her 4th son, she realized that children weren't going to make her husband love her, so she praised God for His gift, for being a part of the Creation story. By her last son, she was fully resigned to abide in God and live on in spite of the negativity around her.

If any woman in the Bible just showed up when she could have given up, it was Leah. Judah was given his name in praise, and Leah's sixth son was named Zebulun, a precious gift. And, while she did hope Jacob would show her honor, she recognized truly where the honor was from.

I am thankful for a loving husband and know that the birth of my baby won't have him love me any more; but I can also learn from Leah Who the precious gift really is from. I can recognize the blessing of being part of the creation story, no matter what any other area of my life is like.

What about you? Have you felt unlovable? Maybe you're in a relationship that isn't healthy, maybe you are in one that's apathetic. Or, maybe, like me you are blessed with a husband that loves you.

No matter the situation or way your baby came about - that baby is a gift. A reason to praise God.

And, no matter what your situation: at work, in the home, with your family, in your own mind, we can learn from Leah's fierceness and show up every day. Show up for us, and for our kids. We can go from the worst to standing on our own in God. That is what truly fierce womanhood is about.

Leah's Prayer

Abba:

There are so many times I feel unloved or unlovable. Or unwanted. Or passed over. Or inconvenient. Or invisible. I have been in times when giving up, curling up in a ball, and throwing in the towel would have been so much easier - or at least seemed as if it would. But, instead of doing that, help me learn the fierce tenacity that Leah had.

May I "show up" in my life each day, no matter what is going on. May I learn to stand totally dependent on You. May I be an example to my child of what that looks like.

Show me, over the next few days, how to take on qualities of all the women in these pages so that I may live a life of fierce womanhood.

Thank you for the examples that have gone before me.

Amen.

Further Reading

Genesis 29-31

RACHEL - JEALOUSY DOES NOT BECOME HER

From Scripture

"Then God remembered Rachel, and God listened to her and opened her womb" - Genesis 30:22

Learning from Rachel

Before this book, Rachel was another woman I felt some contempt for. But, like with Eve, I found my heart softening as I dove into her story for the purposes of this book.

Through much of her story, she is bitter. She is vindictive. She is desperate. She is a thief. She's downright mean and cruel, taunting her sister Leah (another way Leah is so fierce).

Then, I look at her circumstances, and in contrast to her sister, instead of standing in God fiercely, Rachel becomes bitter. And jealous. It does not become her, but it makes sense.

Jacob loved Rachel, but is tricked into taking her sister first, so now she has to share her love. Then, the worst shame for a woman in her time: she is barren. She cannot have children. And, her sister who has "stolen" her love, is now bearing all of his children. Sons, no less. Rachel also sees that despite her hardship, Leah is still turning to God and giving him glory. And, Rachel's heart hardens.

To be honest, I'm not sure I wouldn't have reacted as Rachel did. Sure, I always said I related to Leah, but maybe in her situation, I would have been just as bitter and jealous. During the conception, pregnancy, new momma process, I'm guilty of saying and doing things I was ashamed of and didn't mean, so I can imagine how Rachel felt when nothing was happening for her.

I've been in the position to want a baby and not be ready to have one simply due to life circumstances. I know other mommas have battled infertility and loss. And, when we see happy announcements and family photos, it can be so easy to sink into jealousy and bitterness - *Why me?* or *Why not me? When will it be my turn? My heart aches for that.*

Something I've learned from the story of Leah and Rachel, though, is that we have a choice: to stand fiercely in God, trusting Him, or turning to bitterness. Becoming mean or spiteful. Hiding from the world. Ruining relationships. Demanding things from our partners they have no control to give us. When we act out of our hurt hearts, this can be exactly where we turn.

Instead, let us learn to choose something greater: love and hope.

Because, not only did God "remember" Rachel, but He "listened to her" and "opened her womb". Rachel herself was able to bear Jacob two children - sons. And, without Joseph, who would have been in Egypt to save the sons of Jacob in the famine?

Let's choose love and hope. Hope that God will "remember" us. Hope that God will "listen to" us. And, even if that doesn't happen how we think it should, may we choose love for the women around us. Because healing the heartache only comes forth in love.

Rachael's prayer

Abba:

I very well could fall into the same trap Rachel did, and as Leah did for a time. I could choose bitterness if this motherhood journey hasn't been what I thought it would be. If there have been bumps in the road. I could choose jealousy of those mommas who seem to have it perfect.

Instead, help me choose love and hope. Hope that you will "remember" me and "listen to" me, as you did Rachel. That I would be blessed to be part of the Creation story, my body doing what it was designed to do.

On the other hand, give me compassion for mommas who are in this stage of their motherhood journey - help me remember what it was like when I wanted a child and prayed for a child, but it wasn't time yet.

Give me compassion for those mommas acting out in hurt and anger because they so desperately want a child. May my love and hope be enough to mend the relationship if they are unable to experience it right now.

Thank you for the reminders that love and hope are the way to mend relationships, and that even at our worst or in our brokenness, we are still heard and remembered.

Amen.

Further Reading

Genesis 29-31

TAMAR - A BROKEN PROMISE

From Scripture

"Judah recognized them and said, "She is more righteous than I, since I wouldn't give her to my son Shelah." And he did not sleep with her again." - Genesis 38:26

Learning from Tamar

There are two Tamars in Scripture, and if you get a chance, you should read about them both. They are both fascinating stories of hurt, broken promises, and God's redemption.

We are going to focus on the first Tamar and the life of broken promises made to her. You see, Tamar married a son of Judah. Remember Judah? He's the son of Leah who received the family blessing and is the ancestor of King David & Christ. Tamar had a problem, though. Even though she was trying to live a righteous life and be an honorable wife, she had the unfortunate existence of marrying a dishonorable man who did not do right by her or God. As a matter of fact, he lived a life so displeasing to God, God struck him dead.

Then, came the kinsman redeemer. We'll read more about that later, too, with Ruth. Basically, her husband's brother had to marry her and father a child to sustain the family line. This brother was also dishonorable and "spilled his seed", refusing to honor his commitment as Kinsman Redeemer, so *God did the same thing.*

So, Judah, knowing the law, promised his youngest son (many years her junior) to her, but when he came of age, Judah broke his promise for fear of God killing another son. Well, Tamar took matters into her own hands, dressed as a prostitute and trapped Judah. After finding out about Tamar's pregnancy, Judah was going to have her killed until he realized the child was his. After all of this, Judah recognized that Tamar was the one who had acted righteously. And as a result of all of this? One of *her* twins was in the line of King David and ultimately the line of Christ.

So, why this story? I chose this story for those of us who have to live with broken promises and men who are not honoring God. Chances are, God is not going to strike down your husband or partner who is not honoring Him, but it does put us in a weird position if we are trying to follow God.

God has a purpose for the world: redemption. If we are living with a man who doesn't honor God, our job (short of abuse and infidelity) is to honor our husband, in doing so we honor God. In this way, we show our husbands God's redemption and grace day in and day out.

If we're being honest, this is the way we are supposed to live even if we are living with a Godly man. We are still meant to be an example of God's love and grace.

We become the depiction of righteousness to wayward partners when we live in line with God's word. When we extend forgiveness. When we show grace. W(should be one sentence)hen we love them even when they are unlovable.

It is this example we will also be setting for our children. If our husbands are not leading our households spiritually (which, I pray they all are, but I am not naive enough to believe this book isn't being held by a few of whom I call "pew widows". Women who are standing in the gap, spiritually, for their families), we are meant to be that example to the children we bring into the world. In this way, our husbands and our children will come to know the

God who gives grace.

An important note here: if you're experiencing any kind of abuse, this is an entirely different situation. A husband can be living a life that is apart from God and not be abusive. On the other hand, in the same way a husband who is apart from God can be abusive, so can a man who claims to be walking with God. If abuse is happening, please seek out help. God's covenant as I see it laid out in Ephesians means a man not showing Christ's sacrificial covenant love to his wife has broken the marriage covenant. Seek out spiritual leadership and safety. Your child deserves to know that love is the way we treat one another, not abuse. Seeking help, whether you ultimately stay in the situation or not, is not against what the God of Love and Grace would want for his children. I am not saying definitively to go or to stay, but I am saying - seek guidance, help, and safety. For you and your children.

Tamar's Prayer

Abba:

I want to be righteous in your sight. I want to live an honorable life, one worthy of the call of Christ, as Paul says.

Help me to show my husband and my children the love and grace of Christ every day. Help me to love him, even when he is unlovable, and show my children patience even when my last nerve is fried.

If my husband's heart is far from you, I pray You would draw him to You. Move in his heart, and soften it toward You. If my husband is already close to you, draw his heart even closer day after day.

I pray together we would be an example to our children. An example of being Godly individuals, an example of Godly marriage, and an example of lives surrendered to Your will.

Thank you for this family of mine.

Amen.

Candice Jeneé

Further Reading

Genesis 38

RAHAB - GOD REDEEMS

From Scripture

"Joshua said to the two men who had spied out the land, "Go into the prostitute's house and bring her out and all who belong to her, in accordance with your oath to her"...then, they burned the whole city and everything in it..." - Joshua 6:22, 6:24

Learning from Rahab

Rahab is a fascinating story. A beautiful picture of God's redemption of anyone who will turn to Him. You see, Rahab was not one of God's chosen people, but in her story, God shows us that it's not about nationality or ethnicity, but about where your heart is. Rahab's heart was with Israel's God. She recognized him as the God of gods.

Why did Rahab need redemption? Rahab lived as a foreigner to God's people, a pagan, and living a lifestyle not in line with God's desire. She was part of the world's oldest profession, and her body was used to bring income for her family. However, she also recognized the power and sovereignty of the God of Israel. When Joshua sent spies to Jericho, she saved them. She hid them, protected them, and asked them to remember her. And, that's exactly what God did.

God remembered Rahab and saved her and her family. Then, she became part of God's family, much like Ruth after her. Rahab became one of the two pagan women listed in the genealogy of Christ. Because God is the God of redemption.

I don't know about you, but there are things in my life, like Rahab's life (just definitely not in the same vein as her's), that I'm not proud of. Things that make me so happy that God is a God who redeems. That God's plan includes life, not just death. That redemption is there for all of us, no matter how far we feel we've wandered away from God's grace.

One thing that happened when that strip turned pink is that I realized that I desperately wanted to live a life worthy of the call of Christ, because I wanted to be an example for the baby I was about to bring into this world. That's one of the amazing things about babies. No matter how good of a job you thought you were doing before, they have a way of making you want to be even better.

If you are living in ways you aren't proud of, or you've wandered so far away you're convinced God's grace can't cover you, you're wrong. You can't go too far, and His grace can cover you. Perhaps, see this time of early motherhood as the refining fire. One that brings to light and burns away the things we're not proud of, leaving us closer to our partners and our babies, and our God.

Because, our God is the God that redeems.

Rahab's Prayer

Abba:

Thank you for Your plan of redemption. I know thanks to Eve and Adam we live in a fallen world. Our deepest connection to You and others has been compromised. Thank you for the plan You put in motion to mend the broken connections.

Lord, You see the sins buried in my heart. The ones I know about, and acknowledge, and the ones I don't. You see the sins that others see and the sins they don't. Please, forgive me. Please remove anything from my life that is separating me from You.

I am so glad You are the God of life and not death. The God who forgives, heals, and restores. I pray if any sin is compromising my relationships, you'd remove it. And, if someone else's sin is compromising their relationship with me, that I would show grace as You have shown to me.

I pray my life would be an example to my child of Your redemptive work. That they would understand Your plan to redeem them to Yourself.

Thank you again for the redemptive plan you have for each of us.

Amen.

Further Reading

Joshua 2-3, Joshua 6, Hebrews 11:31, James 2:25

SAMSON'S MOM -
SET APART

From Scripture

"Now see to it that you drink no wine or other fermented drink and that you do not eat anything unclean. You will become pregnant and have a son whose head is never to be touched by a razor because the boy is to be a Nazirite, dedicated to God from the womb. He will take the lead in delivering Israel from the hands of the Philistines." - Judges 13:4-5

Learning from Samson's Mom

I'm impressed by Samson's mom. We don't know her name, but we definitely know her boldness and strength.

God set Samson apart *in the womb* - which means *she* began living set apart before he was even conceived. She lived the life of a Nazirite for her baby, and then raised him that way. From the beginning, she knew the magnitude of motherhood - the impact raising her son would have on her people.

Just like Mary knew the impact having Jesus would have on her people. Neither woman probably fully grasped what was to come and the sacrifice they'd have to make of their child; but both of these strong women knew the magnitude of motherhood.

Along the way, Samson's mom experienced the heartache of a child who chose a different path. A child who lied to her. A child who chose the things of this world over the things of God. However, I want to focus on the time she had him inside of her and beside her, close to her heart.

We are still, today, called to be set apart; therefore, to raise children who are set apart. But, what does that mean for us?

It means that what is said in Psalm 139 still applies today. God knows, intimately, this baby in our womb. He knows every hair on their head and every fuzz on their body. He knows how big or small they will be when placed in our arms for the first time. He knows the number of that baby's days on Earth. And, He has a purpose for that child's life in the world today.

When I sat with this while pregnant, I couldn't help but be moved to tears by the magnitude of it: this precious, blessed surprise was in my belly for a reason. Gifted and entrusted to me for a reason. God decided *I* was the right momma for this particular baby and sent her to me. Just as with Samson's mom,   God decided I was the right one to help raise and guide baby girl to become what He has set out for her to be.

And, like Samson, He knows that ultimately it will be her choice. Like Samson's mom, I will do what I can, but baby girl will make the final choices. I will pray those choices line up with God's Word and His plans of reconciliation, but if she chooses a life more resembling of Samson? Then, I will pray that at the very least, at the very end, her heart will be turned back to him.

It's terrifying and humbling to realize that God chose us for these babies. That He has already set them apart unto Himself, like Samson. That He is entrusting us with their care. That we can do everything right while they are in our womb and in our arms; but, ultimately *they* have to decide. It is terrifying and humbling, and I thank God every day that I merely have to be a loving example. The real burden is on His Spirit to draw her unto Himself.

Samson's Mom's Prayer

Candice Jeneé

Abba:

I am in awe of this task you have placed before me, the magnitude of motherhood. I am amazed that You have chosen me to be the mother of this wonderful little bundle. You could have chosen anyone, but You chose me for this particular baby.

Please, give me the resources I need to raise a child set apart. You have called me to be set apart, which means You have called me to raise a child set apart. Thank you, though, that ultimately the burden falls on You to draw her unto You. As she grows, may her heart be continually pulled toward you in faith, hope, and love.

Thank you for this wonderful call you've given me. I hope I am up to the challenge.

Amen.

Further Reading

Judges 13-16

NAOMI - BITTERNESS
TO JOY

From Scripture

"Don't call me Naomi," she told them. "Call me Mara, because the Almighty has made my life very bitter. I went away full, but the Lord has brought me back empty. Why call me Naomi? The Lord has afflicted me; the Almighty has brought misfortune upon me."
- Ruth 1:20-21

Learning from Naomi

Naomi, when we meet her in Scripture, is well past the new momma phase. She's raised her kiddos and she has survived her husband and both sons. Talk about grief and heart ache, especially in her day and age. In her culture, she basically had nothing.

So, what can we, as new moms, learn from this veteran momma? Well, I see so much to learn from her. Especially as I battle PPD/PPA/PTSD on the daily. Naomi re-named herself in bitterness. She blamed God at first, and literally took on bitterness as her identity.

What I've realized is that sometimes we do the same thing. We take on our feelings or our roles as our *identity.* Have you ever owned a feeling so tightly that it became you? It became how you identify yourself?

During pregnancy, my depression became overwhelming. I am

currently being actively treated for postpartum depression and anxiety, and for the first couple of months there, this seemingly became my identity. Now, I didn't rename myself, but the way it seemingly consumed me and blindsided me, I may as well have. As time has moved on, I have been able to realize I'm not my depression or anxiety, but rather these are simply symptoms of the state I'm in at the moment.

This can happen in other periods of our lives, but it happens in such greater ways when we become mothers. *Why?* Well, first is the hormones. Our bodies just grew a human (or two or three...), they then pushed those babies out (or, well, you know...). Our bodies' nutrients and hormones are out of whack.

Another big reason is: change. That's right. I don't know about you, but baby girl made waves in my life. The most amazing, and beautiful waves, of course, but waves none-the-less. Pregnancy also brought big changes in and of itself.

A third reason this happens in greater numbers in pregnancy and new motherhood is sleep deprivation. I don't know about you, again, but my sleep deprivation began while I was still pregnant. Anyone else have to pee 50 times a night? No? Just me? Or, what about having to actually lift yourself up in order to turn over. No more rolling over in bed.

With all of this hitting at once, it can be easy to make those negative feelings our identity, just like Naomi did. I'd like to use Naomi's story as a cautionary tale: your feelings are just that, feelings. They are temporary, no matter your situation.

I'd also like to learn from Naomi in some positive ways. First, she didn't stay mad at God forever. I learned long ago, God can handle our negative emotions. As long as we keep coming back to Him over and over, we will still have that relationship with our Abba.

Another big thing we, even in our exhausted pregnant or new mom state, can learn from Naomi is giving of ourselves. Even in her darkest moments, Naomi continues to give of herself. She allowed Ruth to stay with her. She opened her heart and home to her daughter-in-law, a foreigner. She taught Ruth about Jewish culture and about the God of gods. She mentored Ruth, encouraged Ruth, and loved Ruth. Even in her suffering, she was open. In our darkest times, in our rough patches, may we still be open, like Naomi.

Now, I cannot leave this chapter without adding an important plea. If you find yourself in the midst of pregnancy or postpartum, and you are overwhelmed by the darkness, the anxiety, the desperation, please, reach out. Get help. You really aren't alone in that. It took me a while to find a place to get help, but I did it. And, I turned to people I was worried about offending with my story, knowing I didn't want to be isolated in the pain and anxiety. They were not offended, and even offered help and hope. Hope is there. Your baby, born yet or not, deserves a momma who is working to become her best, even if you aren't quite there yet. So, I beg of you, don't let this become your identity. Instead, tap into your support system and seek help. It's there, I promise.

Naomi's Prayer

Abba:

This period has been full of mixed emotions. I thought I would only experience joy, but there has also been deep sadness, a lot of tears, and much anxiety. I thought my heart would simply be full, but I have also carried heaviness.

Help me to remember my true identity. Help me to not take this on as my new name. Instead, may I recognize it as a feeling, a reaction to the time and situation I'm in. I pray for sweet sleep when I can get it, and supernatural energy when I can't.

Please surround me with other women, and with the love of my husband and family. Please send the right help my way if needed.

And, please, help me remain open in this time. Help my heart be soft towards others. May I not lose a giving spirit, instead, being gracious to everyone (including myself), as You have been gracious to me.

Thank you for the precious blessing that has created waves in my life. I know nothing will ever be the same again, and I am thankful for that every day.

Amen.

Further Reading

Ruth 1-4

RUTH - ADOPTED IN

From Scripture

"But Ruth replied, "Don't urge me to leave you or to turn back from you. Where you go I will go, and where you stay I will stay. Your people will be my people and your God my God.""- Ruth 1:16

Learning from Ruth

It may seem odd to include a story of adoption in a book about pregnancy, but some mommas become mommas without actually giving birth. And, it was important to me for them to have a chapter, too.

Now, Ruth was an adult when she was "adopted" - I'm of course referring to her becoming a part of God's people.

As we talked about with Rahab, God's issue has never been with race, nationality, gender, etc. God takes issue with people whose hearts are far from Him.

Ruth's heart is not far from Him, though. Quite the contrary. Ruth fully embraces her husband's heritage, his family, and His God. When he dies, she refuses to part from her mother-in-law, instead following Naomi back home.

It is here Ruth's life really changes, she really becomes one of God's people. She is accepted in, she learns and follows the customs, and she serves their God. In doing so, she finds herself in the presence of her Kinsman Redeemer, the one who will take her on to keep the family name alive. Boaz becomes her husband and they have a son, Obed. Obed is the father of Jesse, and Jesse is the father of David. King David. In the line of Christ.

That's right, not only was Ruth adopted in, but she became the ancestor of the Savior of the world.

Mommas who become mommas by adoption are something special. I mean, we are all special, walking this incredible path before us. But to choose to love someone else's child, letting them be a part of your family, giving them access to all of your resources, and making them heirs to what you have? *That is something very special.*

My Grammy became one of the best mommas and is the best Grammy (to grand kids and great grandkids), by choosing to adopt my mom and my uncle, even though she did not give birth to them. Michael and I plan to adopt one day.

There is something powerful about the idea of adoption - it was true in Ruth's day, and it remains so today. Much like Ruth, any of us who have accepted Christ have become a part of God's family. Heirs to everything. Redeemed back to His heart.

Throughout the New Testament, Christ gives us many more illustrations that reflect Ruth's life that remind us of the beauty of being adopted in.

If you are reading this as a momma who has adopted, blessings to you, dear heart. May your love and heart be visible to all who encounter your story. Know, you're not alone. You have chosen a beautiful, painful, and commendable path. You deserve a standing ovation for choosing to love the possibly: unloved, unwanted, and forgotten. *You are a beautiful soul.*

Ruth's Prayer

Abba:

Choosing to love a child that is not yours is so honorable. It's also one of the toughest jobs in the world, as if parenting wasn't hard enough. Give me the strength to live out this role with honor every day.

Thank You for adopting me back into Your family, making me an heir like You did for Ruth. I am so thankful You are the God who redeems and allows us to inherit Your great Kingdom.

Thank you for the child You wove into my heart from day one - no matter how they got to my life. Thank you that their heart is stitched with mine. I pray that no matter how they came to be my child, they would know beyond a shadow of a doubt how fiercely this momma heart loves them.

Thank you for Your love and grace.

Amen.

Further Reading

Ruth 1-4

HANNAH - FOR THIS CHILD I HAVE PRAYED

From Scripture

"I prayed for this child, and the Lord has granted me what I asked of him. So now, I give him to the Lord. For his whole life he will be given over to the Lord." And he worshiped the Lord there." - 1 Samuel 1:27-28

Learning from Hannah

Hannah is one of my favorite women of the Bible. I have read her story so many times and love hearing what others think of her. When we look at Hannah's story, we see:

- A mother's longing
- A mother's heartbreak
- A mother's sacrifice
- A mother's prayer
- A mother's unwavering faith

Hannah's faith is incredible. One of the greatest faiths in the Bible. So much so, she puts her faith in God and promises to turn back to him the greatest gift He would give her.

Any woman who has struggled with infertility would know how difficult the promise Hannah made would be. To gain the child you prayed desperately for and then turn him over to God immediately. She had those first precious years with him, and then turned him over to God's service in the temple. I can only imagine the ache and unwavering faith that would take.

Some see Hannah as desperate, but what I have learned from her is that desperation does not equal a lack of faith. I have been like Hannah, in a way, before. My heart threadbare, crying out before God's throne in tears and making a scene. And, every time I read her story, I am amazed by her faith. My heart breaks right along with her, and I don't question her distraught prayer. I see a woman who is willing to bear her heart: to God and to her husband, and even to the priest. She has no issue with sharing the burden in her heart, revealing her pain and shame.

If you've ever battled infertility, ever ugly cried your prayer at the feet of God, you are not alone. Hannah was there. I have been in similar places - at least in regard to the desperate prayers. I do know what it's like to hope for that pink line only to be disappointed. I know what it's like to have concern that your body isn't and won't do what it's supposed to.

I have been alongside enough women who wait month after month. So, I know you are not alone. And, you don't have to be ashamed of any pain or anguish you feel, any shame you carry, or any desperation you show month after month. Be willing to open your heart: to your husband, to God, to others.

Hannah's story truly reveals the power of prayer and a picture of unwavering faithfulness. But, there is so much more we can learn from Hannah. We can learn what to do when our faithfulness has won out and God has blessed us with children (however that may come about):

• *Prayer for that beloved child.* Before they arrive. While they are growing in our womb (or on their way to us), and once we hold them in our arms and hearts forever. Life may separate us, but our hearts will be linked.

• *Giving the young life back to God.* No matter how we are blessed to become mothers, our child ultimately is God's. He has loaned this precious blessing to us. From Hannah we can learn to give that child right back - no matter what.

Candice Jeneé

- *Love our babies unconditionally.* Hannah loved her son before he was ever born. I have no doubt her heart missed him every day, and she loved him until her death. I can imagine how proud she must have been to see the man of God he grew into, even if apart from her.
- *Always remembering what a precious gift that child is.* Hannah knew her son was a gift from God before he was conceived. Let us also remember that fact about our own children. They are beautiful blessings.

I love Hannah. My heart always connects to her. I want to be a Hannah kind of mom in my own life.

If the life inside of you, or the life you are holding, is born after a struggle or long journey, I encourage you to also be like Hannah in your faith. Be open in your heart. Never be afraid to fall on your face in front of God and ugly cry for that desire of your heart. Have faith that God will bring forth that life. Then, hold that baby close as the precious blessing of God he or she is.

Hannah's prayer

Abba:

Like Hannah, my heart has been broken. And, like Hannah, some have tried to make me ashamed of crying out to you in a messy way. But, life is messy. Even Jesus told us we would have troubles in this life. Life before pregnancy or baby was wonderful, but something felt like it was missing. My heart so desired to be a part of the Creation story in this unique way.

Thank you for the life you allowed to grow in me. Thank you for allowing me to be a mom, partnering with you in such a unique way. I know not every woman gets the opportunity. My journey may have been short to motherhood, or long, but I am looking forward to filling this role. I am so blessed that you chose me for my baby.

May I always remember what a precious gift he/she is. May my heart continue to be moved to prayer - for this child I have prayed. Lord, that my heart would be turned to you in sacrifice, knowing this child is not mine, but yours. A beautiful loan you have given me. May I never take that responsibility lightly, but instead instill an unwavering faith and love for you into my baby. Thank you for the opportunity to love this precious soul.

Amen.

Further Reading

1 Samuel 1-2

BATHSHEBA - THE RAINBOW BABY

From Scripture

"Then David said to Nathan, "I have sinned against the Lord." Nathan replied, "The Lord has taken away your sin. You are not going to die. But because by doing this you have shown utter contempt for the Lord, the son born to you will die."" - 2 Samuel 12:13-14

Learning from Bathsheba

Anguish. Heartbreak. Devastation. Anger. Grief. Disbelief.

Imagine a scenario with me, if you will. It's springtime. A war is happening and your husband, who you love, is off to war. You are at your home, bathing and enjoying time to yourself, maybe missing your husband greatly.

Then, you are summoned by the King, the most powerful man in the land. *But, shouldn't he be away at war? What is he doing here?* He lets you know he has to have you. There is no explicit threat, but you know that denying a King is grounds for death, and you are a woman after all. So, you allow the King to have his way.

Then, you're late...there's a baby coming and your husband is gone. So, the King brings him home, especially to see you. But, you married an honorable man, acting much more honorably than the King. He refuses to sleep with you, won't even go inside your house, until all the men come home. So, the King has him killed, sending him to the front lines carrying his own death sentence. Once your husband is dead, the grief still fresh in your heart, the King takes you as his wife. For his dishonorable conduct, you give birth to a baby who dies days later.

Anguish. Heartbreak. Devastation. Anger. Grief. Disbelief.

I can only imagine these and so many others are felt by Bathsheba as she lays her baby to rest. I talked to my husband about this and told him I don't know how Bathsheba found grace in her heart after this loss. I can only imagine carrying my baby to term and losing her. And, for it to be his fault? I don't know that I could get over it.

Yet, Bathsheba does. When we read their story further, it's clear after this that David and Bathsheba actually have a good marriage; and it is her son, not his oldest, who becomes the next King of Israel.

This baby was her rainbow baby. I am in awe of women who have these rainbow babies. I can only imagine what it's like to lose your baby. To know them by feeling or even hold them, and then they are gone. I've been to the funeral of a baby who was mere days old. It's heartbreaking.

I don't know if I could do it, though. Have another after death. I'd like to think I could. There is a beauty to mommas of rainbow babies. A tenacity. A fierce love and devotion. It's beautiful to see the blessing they find in their babies. The next pregnancy is full of mixed emotions: joy and anxiety, love and fear. I have seen it time and again in women I've sat with who have experienced this kind of loss.

Today, I'm mostly speaking to those mommas who have experienced this loss. It's a unique and deeply gutting experience. Since miscarriage, still birth, and infant loss is greater than we know, I really wanted those mommas to know *they are not alone.* Even *their* story is in the Bible, another momma knows how they feel, and that momma's rainbow baby went on to be the wisest man in history. Bathsheba held a special place in David's heart, in her son's heart, and in the heart of God. She is honored alongside her first husband in the lineage of Jesus.

I don't know why God allows us to lose these precious gifts in the earliest days and weeks of their existence. We will never know this side of heaven, but just know you are not alone. This rainbow baby you carry or hold is a beautiful, blessed gift. And, just like Solomon, God's got big plans for this little human.

Bathsheba's Prayer

Abba:

Thank you for each of my babies. The ones I've gotten to hold, and the ones I only hold in my heart. You understand the loss of a child more than anyone. You gave up your Son, so I know you understand the sting and ache in my heart. I know you don't fault me for the anger, the devastation, the confusion, or the grief.

In this period with my sweet rainbow baby, I know you don't fault me for the fear and anxiety. For holding on so tightly, and maybe even keeping it a secret until I know we're "clear". I place this baby in Your hands. You have big plans for this little human, and I feel so blessed to be a part of their journey.

Please, heal the past hurt. I know the loss will never be erased from my mind, but may the sting lessen with time. May the hope of meeting my baby in eternity keep me going. May the love and laughter of this rainbow baby keep my heart soft and tender, able to love always.

Thank you for keeping me going in the darkest days. Thank you for your blessings.

Amen.

Further Reading

2 Samuel 11-12,

ELIZABETH - SUPPORTING OTHER MOMMAS

From Scripture

"Both of them were righteous in the sight of God, observing all the Lord's commands and decrees blamelessly. But they were childless because Elizabeth was not able to conceive, and they were both very old." - Luke 1:6-7

Learning from Elizabeth

Elizabeth is a wonderful momma. I loved re-reading her story for this book. She's not shown much in the Gospels, but what we do see is a massive support for other mommas, especially her cousin Mary. We also see a woman who is strong in faith - and possibly one of the first filled with the Holy Spirit. A note from my research - Elizabeth is such a righteous and honorable woman, she is even honored in Muslim tradition! Talk about a righteous woman.

From what I gather, even before her pregnancy, Elizabeth was a strong woman, full of faith and hope. Until her pregnancy with John (as in, John the Baptist), she was barren in a time when barrenness was frowned upon. But, even in that state, she seems to be content in the life God had given her. However, when she finds out about her son, she also recognizes the blessing of the Lord, giving praise where praise is due. She knows her son is a gift. When telling her husband about her baby, the angel told him that God sees him and Elizabeth as righteous people. It must run in the family.

Once she was pregnant, she fit into the role of momma so well. Her embrace of this new life stage opened her up to be supportive of Mary in her pregnancy, as well, even if Mary's was one that could result in death - being she wasn't married. Elizabeth showed love and support, and so did her unborn son.

Much like Samson's mom (and Mary), Elizabeth's baby was explicitly set apart from the beginning. I have no doubt she loved and raised her son in that way, since she was already described as righteous before God.

During this time, once Mary knew she was pregnant, she went to visit Elizabeth. I don't know if Elizabeth knew about Mary's baby, but when John leapt within her, she sure did. And, that is where her incredible and humble support begins.

Pregnancy and motherhood is not a journey easily walked alone. I am fairly certain I would not have made it without the support of others. One of my best friends was pregnant at the same time I was, and due to my baby girl deciding she wanted to greet the world a few weeks early, our baby girls were born mere days apart. What a blessing that was as part of my journey.

It is my prayer that you are not entering this role alone. It's my prayer that you have an Elizabeth in your life. Someone who encourages you, supports you, and picks you up when you're down. It's also my prayer that you become an Elizabeth for others. We may not all agree on how to be pregnant or how to be a parent, but as long as our babies are loved and raised in God's family, I fully believe there is a lot of margin for grace. The amount of mom-shaming in the world is horrible, but you won't find that here.

And, you wouldn't have found that with Elizabeth.

I hope this book helps me serve as an Elizabeth for you. I also hope it inspires you to find other Elizabeths in your life, and to become an Elizabeth for others.

Elizabeth's prayer

Abba:

Thank you for this precious gift inside me, no matter how long it took or how surprised I was. You have truly blessed me with this baby. I know this baby is meant for a purpose, just like John was. You already know this baby's name, number of hairs, and future.

Thank you for all of the support you have surrounded me with. If I don't have much support, or am keeping myself in fear, please send a supportive group and the confidence to reach out. I also pray that I would be like Elizabeth for someone else.

Just like Elizabeth was righteous before you, and a source of encouragement to others, please teach me how to be that. I know that this is one part of life that is not easily walked alone, and I don't want anyone to have to do so. May I be the one that that can be there if someone needs it.

Thank you that we are each blessed among women to be carrying this precious bundle inside of us and then hold them in our arms.

Thank you for being the ultimate support in this journey, never leaving us, sending Your Spirit to be our comforter and guide.

Amen.

Further Reading

Luke 1

MARY - THY WILL BE DONE

From Scripture

"I am the Lord's servant," Mary answered. "May your word to me be fulfilled." Then the angel left her." - Luke 1:38

Learning from Mary

If ever there was a momma who walked in confidence, it was Mary. Before starting this book, I used to think of Mary as a timid little girl, considering she would have been between 14-16 when she carried and gave birth to Jesus. As I've re-read and researched, though, I realize, she is bold, confident, and is the most willing heart.

She was a teen and unmarried mom in a time when being an unmarried mom could have caused death. She knew carrying her baby was a call of God, so she said Thy will be done, knowing she was going against culture. Knowing it could lead to her death.

Mary was anything but meek and weak. I can only imagine she would have to be tough and confident to be the mother of God. Imagine when they found Jesus in the temple after he'd been missing for three days and he says, "woman, don't you know..." How would you as a momma handle that? I'm pretty sure she reacted like many mothers would. Something like, *"you may be the Son of God, but I'm your mother; and you had me worried."*

Now, maybe it didn't go quite like that, but when we see her in scripture, I can tell she doesn't cow-tow to others. She speaks up for what she believes in, she loves all of her children, and she is one tough cookie. She would have to be to referee sibling brawls between Christ and his siblings. (Imagine what that would have been like). It is also possible she was widowed early, so, at some point, she was back to doing all this mothering flying solo.

Through it all, she turns to God and says, "Thy will be done", even when watching her Son give the ultimate sacrifice on the cross and feeling her heart break in a million pieces.

Being a teen or unmarried mom is not an easy role in any society, so when a girl today makes the decision to own her consequences and have her baby, she is also in essence telling God "Thy will be done". And, while I'm not focusing here on the teen and unwed mommas, they have a place too; and are blessed among women with the gift they carry inside them. They deserve love and grace, too.

That said, what I'd like to focus on here, is the willingness to say, "Thy will be done". Shortly after baby girl was born, I stated, *motherhood is the biggest test in letting go of control and trusting God.* It really is true. To survive this whole motherhood thing, we each have to say daily "Thy will be done." We never know when something is going to change. We never know if we will outlive our children and feel our heart break irreversibly. We never know if an incident will occur and we have to care for our baby for the rest of our lives. We never know if our little one will one day grow up and turn away, like Samson, again, having our heart break in many pieces. We. Never. Know.

But, God knows. God knows His plan for our child, and He knows the choices our child will make. Therefore, like Mary, from the time we find out we are carrying our baby until the day we leave this Earth, the cry of our heart in this whole event of motherhood has to be *Thy will be done.*

Mary's Prayer

Abba:

From the moment that test showed a baby inside me, I realized I have no control here. I strive for control always, but this is one area it will never happen. Help me learn to trust you in ways I have never been able to before. Help me to truly learn to cast my anxiety on You, trusting that You care for me and my baby.

Lord, Thy will be done here, because I don't know what the future holds. Thank you for whatever time I have with this baby, whether it's only a few weeks in the womb, or all the rest of my days, or anywhere in between. Thank You for this precious life.

Daily, help me relinquish control to You, trusting You to see Your will done in my child's life, and in my life as his/her momma. Thank you for trusting me to be the momma to raise this baby. I pray I won't let You down, even on days I fall short.

Lord, You are in control, always. Everything is in Love, for Your Glory.

Thy will be done.

Amen.

Further Reading

Matthew 1-2, Luke 1-2

FINAL THOUGHTS-
DAY 17

Taken Blessed Broken Given

Several times in the New Testament we see Jesus doing this exact process:

Taking. Blessing. Breaking. Giving.

But, it isn't just food he does this to. He does this with us.

It is extremely obvious in pregnancy and motherhood. We are taken into His plan - becoming part of the Creation process itself. It's a blessing to be invited in this way. We are blessed with this child we care for. But, so often, pregnancy and motherhood comes with brokenness - the result of the fall. Weak bodies, loss, difficulty, watching children struggle and suffer, complete and utter reliance on God, allowing them their own choices and the consequences of those (just as God does for us).

It is only in being taken, blessed, and broken that we can be given in this life of motherhood. It is only in being taken, blessed, and broken we are able to be given in general.

Over time, God has been showing me what I'm to do with what He's walked me through - and why. And, this is part of that.

First, He placed teens on my heart. Then, He has grown that very specifically into teen girls & women. I believe that's why He blessed me with a baby girl. It's all about the *why* He's awakened in me.

For each of us in this journey, just like all the women in these pages, God has chosen us to be part of this Creation story. God has blessed us with our little bundles, and even with our brokenness. And, he has/is bringing us through our brokenness.

This way we can be given in marriage/relationships, in our pregnancy, and in our motherhood.

It is this knowledge and message that has sparked this book. It's what propelled me through the hardship of pregnancy. It's the knowledge that had me so excited for every move, kick, jab I felt inside me, and made me ecstatic to meet the beautiful little girl God sent me.

Final thoughts:

"I feel like I'm the only one."

"Tell me I'm not alone."

"Is this normal?"

"What do I do?"

I wanted to be in love with pregnancy. I wanted it to go ok. I wanted to enjoy the whole process; but, honestly, that wasn't the case for me.

I am extremely thankful for a healthy baby and viable pregnancy. But, the process has been extremely tough on my personal health and mental health.

Yet God really has shown me that this is a connecting experience. A defining experience to become what He called me to. It's a turn on the path like many of these women experienced. Most of us have a turning point moment - it can be a day, a second, a month, a year.

How is God maneuvering you in this time? How is this time affecting you and your family?

My hope is by hearing the stories of these women in the bible. Hearing my story, going deeper into scripture helps you become the daughter of the King, the wife, the mother you desire to be. My prayer is it helps ease anxiety, soften loneliness, and inspires love.

APPENDIX

List of Quick Reference Verses for Pregnancy and Early Motherhood

- Isaiah 49:25
- Joshua 1:5,9
- 1 Samual 16:7
- Philippians 4:6-8
- Proverbs 3:5-6
- Psalm 28:7
- 2 Corinthians 9:8
- Isaiah 40:11,31
- 1 Peter 5:7
- Psalm 139
- Psalm 112:7
- Psalm 127:3-4
- Psalm 22:9-10
- James 1:17-18
- Isaiah 26:3-4
- 2 Corinthians 12:8-10
- Philippians 4:13
- Colossians 3:1-2
- Isaiah 66:9
- 2 Chronicles 16:9
- Isaiah 54:10
- Psalm 46:1

- Psalm 27:1
- Psalm 53:18-22
- Psalm 73:26
- Ephesians 2:14
- Zechariah 4:10

www.ingramcontent.com/pod-product-compliance
Lightning Source LLC
Chambersburg PA
CBHW020605030426
42337CB00013B/1225